I DECIDE

I Decide

The Happy Little Guide to Living Your Best Life

Lisa Cox & Erin Lopez

All Rights Reserved. No portion of this book may be reproduced, stored in a retrieval system, or transmitted in any form or by any means-electronic, mechanical, photocopy, recording, scanning, or other-except for brief quotations in critical reviews or articles without the prior permission of the author.

Published by Game Changer Publishing

Paperback ISBN: 979-8-9870839-4-9
Hardcover ISBN: 979-8-9877531-6-3
Digital ISBN: 979-8-9880752-0-2

www.GameChangerPublishing.com

DEDICATION

We give thanks always to our Lord for every day and every opportunity. And a special thank you to our mentors for leading us on our successful path in life.

We want to personally thank our friends and confidants Shannon Ryan, Justin Prince, Dale Smith Thomas, Tanya and Chris Carr, Breanna Michel, Lisa McGuire, Tony Zolecki, Michelle Haas Henkensiefken, Margie Aliprandi, John Melton and Michelle Barnes for sharing their stories and testimonies that moved us with every word.

And to our husbands and children who supported this movement from day one and constantly push us to be better. And finally to each other, for making each other laugh until we cry, for countless hours on the phone and zoom, and for our friendship and partnership to change the world together.

DOWNLOAD YOUR FREE GIFTS

Read This First

Just to say thanks for buying and reading our book, we would like to give you a few free bonus gifts, no strings attached!

To Download Now, Visit:

www.IDecideBook.com/Freegifts

I DECIDE

The Happy Little Guide to Living Your Best Life

Lisa Cox & Erin Lopez

www.GameChangerPublishing.com

Foreword

"I Decide," what a perfect title for a "guide" to help you to live "your best life."

Why is this the perfect title? Because "I decide" is literally the very first step and the pivotal moment where your entire life can change. All change begins with a decision.

Even the root origin of the word "decision" confirms this. "Decision" comes from the Latin root "cision" which means "to cut," and "de" which means "off." An "incision" would "cut in," and a "decision" would "cut off." What are you "cutting off"? All other possibilities. When you come to a fork in the road, and you make a "decision" to go right, you cut off all possibilities of going left.

As you begin reading this masterfully written book and your journey to *live your best life*, consider this, every decision that you have ever made in your entire life, every single one, has led you to these words in this book at this specific moment. My friend, you have made an appointment to be here. The question for you is simply, what will you decide to do with all the inspiration, mentorship, and wisdom that you will glean as you read this book? The power is in your hands and in what *You Decide* next.

Speaking of mentorship, your decision to begin reading this book and embarking on this journey is coming with the priceless mentorship of two incredible women, Lisa Cox and Erin Lopez. I consider myself fortunate to know both very well. Simply put, they are first-class in every area of life. While the first step to living "your best life is to "decide," step two is to run to mentors you can model and learn from. Mentors like this will help you continue to make the right decisions. Lisa Cox and Erin Lopez are both uniquely qualified to be that mentor and model you can follow.

They are first-class women. They lift and inspire people. They are not catty or mean. They are secure in who they are and the value they bring to the world. They are classy and kind.

They are first-class in their marriages. They have created marriages that anyone would admire and aspire to be like. They are faithful, strong, wise, and loyal. They have raised beautiful families. They are a model for how to raise confident, capable, and courageous children.

They are first-class in fitness and health. You cannot be around either of these women and not feel how vibrant and alive they both are. They are physically strong. They are athletic. They "walk the walk." They are cognizant of the foods that they have put in their bodies. Their commitment to health and fitness has allowed them to truly "live their best lives" and for us to learn and model them.

They are first-class businesswomen. I have had the opportunity to watch them build a multimillion-dollar business and lead tens of thousands of people. I've seen them dig in and lead through challenging times, and I've watched them scale and lead through good times. I've watched them stay relevant year in and year out, never succumbing to being the type of person who talks about what they "used to do." I've watched them be emotionally mature and wise through very challenging situations. I've watched them be reliable and consistent. I've watched them in quiet moments with only one or two people, and I have watched light up big stages with thousands watching. These women are the real deal.

My friend, you should be congratulated. You have made the right decision to pick up and read this book. You have made the decision to pick credible and proven mentors. The next step is yours. Be the one that when you look back on your life that you can say, "I decided," the life I created vs. just responding to the life that came at you.

I am so excited for you and am personally honored to turn you over to the capable and trusted wisdom of two of the most capable and powerful women I know, Lisa Cox and Erin Lopez.

– **JUSTIN PRINCE,** Family Man, Entrepreneur, International Speaker, Author

Table of Contents

Introduction 1

Chapter 1 – The Mindset Ripple.. 5

Chapter 2 – Excuse Me!! 17

Chapter 3 – Weight for it!... 25

Chapter 4 – Mo Money Honey! 35

Chapter 5 – Say Cheese!... 43

Chapter 6 – Get Outta My Way!.. 49

Chapter 7 – Circle of Trust... 57

Chapter 8 – No Drama Mama! 63

Chapter 9 – That's A Wrap.. 71

Introduction

Buckle up, Buttercups!

Have you been able to make the decisions necessary to live the life you've always dreamt of? Are there things that have happened to you in your life that have you paralyzed in fear? Are you too comfortable in your own ways? Are there words in your head that you can't stop hearing? Are there people in your life who are suffocating you? Can you visualize what you want but can't seem to get there?

This is your time. This is your way out. This is the book that will help you escape your past and break free to the next level—The level and the life you deserve. No matter your age, your profession, your gender, or your race, this book is for you.

In the pages ahead, you will hear from both Erin and Lisa as they make you laugh, cry, and give you the tools, the power and determination to DECIDE your future. The one big promise we make to you is that by finishing this book, you will have opened your heart to do some real soul-searching to understand why you are stuck where you are and how to get yourself unstuck.

Roll up your sleeves or kick off your high heels and let's get to work on your most important investment, YOU.

Erin is a wife, a mother and entrepreneur behind *A Lopez Lifestyle*. A much sought after speaker, author and leader in the direct sales industry, she brings passion, humor and a great pair of shoes with her career. Erin has more than 25 years of experience in the fashion industry. She was discovered as a young model, and her career took her to big cities, creating big dreams. She worked her way up to the top of the fashion industry as a coveted modeling agent in Chicago before hanging up her four-inch heels to get married and raise a family. She met her amazing husband, who brought her to the Midwest and became a "bonus" mom to a son while quickly adding two girls to their coveted crew. Like many moms, she couldn't ignore the "itch" to find something that would allow her to have the ability to raise a family and have a career. She was able to marry her passions of fashion and family, starting her own high-profile wardrobe styling business, eventually leading her to the industry of network marketing. She has proven that it is possible to have time and financial freedom and now shows others how to do the same.

She has since built a multimillion-dollar business, graced countless stages telling her story and continues to build a business to help others have success and confidence, all while dressing chic (albeit mostly now she calls it "comfy chic") while working from her home office or on the phone. She currently lives in Houston, Texas, with her husband, two teenage girls and two Goldendoodles.

Lisa Cox is the CEO of *Live Clean Lisa* and is well known throughout the home-based direct sales and social retail industry for her experience, knowledge and passion for improving the lives of others. She's been married for 33 years to a wonderful man who moved her from her California life to the Midwest, where she fell in love with the four seasons and the kindness and hearts of her community in Springfield, Missouri. Lisa started in real estate and found her love of sales but quickly learned she wanted to seek time freedom and landed in the direct sales/home base business world. She flourished, having the flexibility to raise their two beautiful and successful daughters and to motivate and inspire others to chase their ultimate financial and time freedom.

Serving others quickly became her passion, being the example you can set to reach huge personal and professional goals and still be a present and engaged parent and spouse. Lisa was introduced to the direct sales industry and started selling products she loved in 1996, making it her full-time career in 2000. She's a multimillion-dollar earner and a student advocate for health, fitness and clean living. She specializes in helping others build teams and grow themselves while earning an income from their home and phones.

Lisa was featured in the book *Miracle Morning for Network Marketers* by Hal Elrod and is a popular stage speaker and success trainer. Her top goal is to lead by example in maintaining balance in her own life while helping others be the entrepreneurs of their entire lives.

Erin and Lisa are co-authors of the best-selling book, *Social Impact: 31 Social Media Strategies Guaranteed To Explode Your Network Marketing Business,* a compilation of professionals in today's business who have come together to bring you the top strategies they use to build 6, 7, and 8-figure Network Marketing businesses.

~ 1 ~

The Mindset Ripple

"You cannot have a positive life and a negative mind"
- **Joyce Meyer**

We've all heard the saying, "mindset matters." But why? Mindset ultimately means how we process and keep processing events throughout our lives. If we grew up poor, our mindset could choose to accept we will always be poor. We have failed at losing weight countless times, so we think we will always fail despite hopes that this time will finally work. We haven't had a wildly successful career after several attempts, so we think we will never make it to the top—it's not going to happen. As children, we've watched marriages around us fall apart. So now we think our own marriages will most likely fail. Our mindset chooses to see how the future will continue to look. Things happen to us because it's how we expect them to happen. It is all we know. It's how our mind perceives events and chooses to look at the future. We don't know another route. So how can we expect the future to look different than our minds perceive?

What if we decided to look at things differently?

What if we took a ride together to bring you to the place of not allowing our past mindset to affect our future?

We can have two types of mindsets—*fixed* or *growth*. Which one do you think you are? With a *fixed* mindset, our decisions, thoughts and even our intelligence are static, meaning we are not open to other possibilities. You have heard the saying, "It is what it is," or another common response, "These are the cards I was dealt." With a fixed mindset, these are common examples of accepting a situation as it is. We'd rather avoid the situation than face it head-on because we have already decided we can't change the outcome. What's the point? Do any of the following examples sound familiar or ring true in your own life? Does your family's health history pre-determine your thoughts of your own health and hold you back from deciding to be different?

How about the way your parents raised you financially, and because of that, you have chosen to put a mental cap on your own financial situation, not just for the current day but for the future. You may have grown up in an unhappy home filled with negative words and a "glass half empty" mentality, and now you carry that over into your own family.

What's interesting is that most times, with a fixed mindset, we don't even know that we allow this to happen. I can't help but think of my own experience with a fixed mindset that could have changed the course of my life and countless other lives I have served along the way. When I was introduced to network marketing, I was not only very closed-minded about it, I ran in the opposite direction. *You want me to host a home party and ask others to buy something I just pulled out of my back seat? No, thank you.* I was used to a large salary with a beautiful view of downtown Chicago. The thought of telling my friends and family, much less myself, that I had joined a direct sales business gave me the sweats. I'll never forget meeting a tall, blonde, beautiful woman at a friend's house who was dressed to a "T" but also one of the most accomplished, kindest women I had met in my 20-year career.

We instantly clicked, and I learned she was a successful stay-at-home mom who made millions in the direct sales business. I listened to her tell me about her career, which sparked my curiosity since I had only known one path to success. I don't think she had my Chicago view, but she surely could visit anytime she wanted with her financial success and freedom. *Maybe there was something to having an open mind to an industry I knew nothing about.* We parted ways after that night, stayed friends over the years, and while I educated myself on the industry, I slowly opened my closed mind to the possibility of taking my future into my own hands. Don't worry, I'm not hosting parties at my neighbor's house, but I am a part of the social retail model that changed how we shop before the whole world changed itself. And the best part, that woman I mentioned earlier, is not only the other voice you are listening to in this book, but she is also one of my closest and dearest friends and an even better business partner.

A fixed mindset could have closed the door to our wildly successful partnership and the thousands of others we have served and continue to serve.

The opposite of a fixed mindset is a *growth* mindset. Personally, it took us years to understand what this actually meant. We were making decisions from a growth mindset without even realizing it. You can see that a closed door is actually a window. A growth mindset recognizes the low points and setbacks as teaching moments. A growth mindset understands that if you get a flat tire, you don't slash the other three or buy a new car. A growth mindset takes on challenges, looks for solutions, and utilizes talents, abilities and intelligence to develop through effort and practice.

Friends, this journey has been a marathon, not a sprint. We have learned to persevere through setbacks, embrace the process of learning while worrying less about the outcome, and find inspiration in others' success.

We want to share our friend Chris' story in his own words.

I was a senior in high school, and my classmates and I were going to a career fest. That is where a number of colleges gather with information about their institutions in hopes of getting students to want to attend. Our class was gathered in the library, and keep in mind it was a very small town with very low aspirations. The high school counselor asked the question, "What do you want to be?" There were many different answers. I raised my hand and said that I wanted to play professional basketball. She told me, "Oh, Chris, you can't honestly think you can do that for a living? You should focus on attending a good trade school and learning a trade. The odds of making money playing basketball are one in a million!" The actual number back in 1991 was one in every 990,000, so she was close.

When I heard these words, I made a strong inner decision that I would not allow what other people thought to direct my path in life. What I heard that day was 1.) You are not good enough. 2.) You will never be good enough. 3.) You will never amount to anything. I wrote those words on a piece of paper and taped it in my locker. Those would be the words that instead ended up driving and pushing me forward the most. I took that same paper with me when I signed my National Letter of Intent to play basketball at SIU-Carbondale. It also followed me when I left school for the NBA draft after my junior year. It was with me when I was drafted and signed my first contract with the Phoenix Suns in 1995. It accompanied every stop that I had during a nine-year professional basketball playing career, along with another 19+ years in the profession, including starting a company, finishing my college degree, and becoming a Division 1 assistant coach.

As I stated earlier, I have been involved in basketball for 27+ years now. I still allow those same words from high school to drive me toward my goals and aspirations of becoming a collegiate head coach. A lot of hard work has *been done, and there is still plenty more to do. My decision not to allow other people's influence and words to define my future ultimately changed my mindset and path in life.*

We get chills knowing this incredible man and his decision and strong growth mindset created a massive ripple effect around him. He is an amazing father and coach who positively influences everyone he meets.

Once we can identify the different mindsets, we can see a clear distinction between those with a fixed mindset and those with a growth mindset. In her book, *Mindset: The New Psychology of Success,* Carol S. Dweck, Ph.D. says, "Out of these two mindsets, which we manifest from a very early age, springs a great deal of our behavior, our relationship with success and failure in both professional and personal contexts and ultimately our capacity for happiness."

Here's another story of our friend Dale and her incredible resilience in fighting against a fixed mindset. Dale grew up in a poverty-stricken area of north Mississippi. She lived on a farm 10 miles out in the country from the nearest town, Yupura, Mississippi, which has a population of fewer than 2,000 people. She grew up very shy, and insecure, and as she looks back now, she can say that she was very negative. Dale said, "I had no vision for my future, and I didn't even dare to dream I could have a future. My sweet mama wanted me to get married and have some children and live close by." Well, living so far out in the country, it was hard for this shy girl to get a date, much less a husband. We'll let Dale pick up the story from here.

As graduation approached, my one boyfriend in high school broke up with me and broke my heart. I am pretty sure he broke my mother's, also. He was Dale Thompson. Yes, you read that right. We were precious. Dale and Dale. During my high school years, I realized that I possibly had options. I could change my attitude. Maybe it was not my conditions that determined my destiny. Maybe it was my own decisions. So because of my mentor and some great teachers in high school, I decided to be the first person in my family to attend college. That was a big deal in my family. My daddy had not even graduated from high school. I didn't know how I could go to college because we didn't have the money. However, deep in my soul, I knew the "what" had to come before the "how." I decided I wanted to attend college and just had faith that the "how" would appear.

After college, I realized it was up to me; no one was coming to rescue me. There was even a book at the time called Prince Charming is Not Coming. I had to do the hard work to earn the lifestyle I wanted. I decided I would work hard to be my own Prince Charming. As the financial reality of college was crashing down on me, a miracle happened—at least, that is what I'm calling it. During this time, an elderly woman passed away in my community. She and her husband donated all the timber rights on their property as a scholarship fund for anyone in the surrounding counties where they owned land to attend college for free. That one decision has now put more than $118,000,000 into education in Mississippi. The Sumner Foundation has changed so many lives over generations, and they are the reason I have a degree from Mississippi State University. I did not know them personally, but their decision rippled out and changed my life. We never know how one decision can be the catalyst not only for our lives but the lives of others.

I look around at my life and the blessings that surround me. I look at my bookshelf at the two books I have written and published—one became a best seller. I look at the awards for my speaking career. I look at the crown I was given when I was Miss Tennessee. I look at an award from a speaking engagement in Asia. I see a photo with Dr. Phil when I was a guest expert on his show. But even more importantly, I see my reflection in my big computer *screen of a once shy, scared, unsure young woman who dared to dream and took the risk to decide to have a bigger life. Who I have become on this journey is so much bigger than what I have achieved. I learned not to let my challenges in life define me. This girl who would not raise her hand in class now has stood on a stage speaking to an audience of more than 15,000. That's more than seven times the number of people in my hometown! My mindset now is that whatever you face in life, you must decide to **grow** through it and not just **go** through it.*

Dale's growth mindset story has not only affected her own life, but can you imagine the countless people her faithful decision inspired?

"History, despite its wrenching pain, cannot be unlived, but if forced with courage, need not be lived again" - Maya Angelou

What has happened in your life to create your current mindset? Job loss, divorce, tragedy, limited resources, a death, health problems, illness, weight struggles, depression, marital struggles, missed opportunity, lack of support system, or just a really bad day?

Let's take a deep dive together. We have all had a time in our life that may have done damage and affected how we think and react. Sadly, most people won't deal with this or change until something tragic or major happens. Are you the type that ignores your situation instead of facing it head-on and drawing a line in the sand? Did an event or a person dictate your response to trying to improve yourself? It is a tale as old as time to let what your family did or what someone said to you affect the way you make decisions in our family.

Our parents struggled with their marriage. Between the two of them, they had eight marriages. As the children of that upbringing, my sisters and I could have decided that it's normal to divorce or throw away a marriage at the first signs of trouble. Regardless of their struggles in marriage, they were amazing and strong parents who taught us to fight for love with the hope we would learn from their mistakes and find ourselves in long, healthy and happy marriages. Subsequently, all three girls have been married to our first and only husbands for 31, 32 and 33 years.

This year (2023), we fondly look back at our parents' lives as lessons in love and don't take any of the negative or bad with us. That decision, at times, was a challenge, but it has served us so much better than lamenting over what could have been. We see it as a life tool and choose to live differently.

> **Say this with us:** *"I decide to rewrite my family history, break the chains of the past, and I decide that my past will not dictate my future."*

We say, STOP! Why are you waiting? Don't wait for something tragic or an event to make the necessary changes for your happiness. Do it now. Get yourself in the modus operandi of NOW, not someday. Shake yourself and say, *I deserve better.* Trust us! WE KNOW YOU DO!

Let's start with you. Do you always tell people about the glorious decisions you are making to improve your life by losing weight, getting out of debt, or fixing your attitude? But then you immediately fall back on old programming two days later. Think of the New Year's resolution trap. A New Year's resolution is a tradition mostly in the Western world, in which a person resolves to continue good practices, change an undesired trait or behavior, accomplish a personal goal, or otherwise improve that behavior.

But statistically (according to a *Forbes* magazine study), 80% of resolutions are broken and discarded by February.

To make definitive decisions to get you solidly on a path to healthy change, you need to be the first one who believes in you. Don't let the words roll off your tongue without your brain backing it up with a resounding, *I am doing this right this time! I believe in myself!* Even if you don't, the trend of non-supporters and non-believers will change, but it starts with YOU, proving it to YOU first.

TRACK IT, BABY, TRACK IT!

Next is to track all activities and celebrate small steps and wins along the way. According to research published in *The Huffington Post*, you become 42% more likely to achieve your goals and dreams simply by writing them down regularly. Just the act of writing down your dreams and goals ignites ideas and productivity in the powerhouse that is your subconscious mind. Buy the stinking notebook already or grab one from your drawer and get writing. Just imagine, in football, with the above statistic, you could already be standing at the 42-yard line on your way to scoring a touchdown by simply tracking your goals. You are that much closer to the end zone! Let's GO!

Why would we track our progress? Good news! We're here to tell you.

1. **Milestones** are crucial and tell you if your efforts are working. They are also benchmarks to see improvements and give you the feedback you need to keep the path or reset your plan.

2. **Creating a Baseline** offers a way to measure how much progress you've made and compare the effectiveness of different strategies along the way.

3. **The psychological factor.** If you are trying to change a habit, you must make sure you know your feelings and attitude daily. If you want to change your spending, you need to track where your dollars are spent each day. If you buy a $7 fancy coffee each day, you may not even be aware of that money spent. Making lists will show you exactly where you spend and where you can cut to achieve your spending goals and keep your budget healthy.

4. **Prove it to yourself.** Having a detailed record of what you have been up to can come in handy; your success will shine from the paper or point to areas to improve.

5. It will point to **recurring problems** for which you can then find a solution so you can keep trucking towards your goals.

Itty bitty milestones are magic, friends!

Most decisions, like our Resolution trap, are bailed on because they are too severe and too much at once. For example, a person who does no physical activity and says, *I'm going to run 5 miles a day*, will most likely burn out quickly or get injured. The key is to make small attainable goals and do the big "ta-da" in the mirror every time you reach one; then do it again with another small attainable goal. Otherwise, the disappointment of not hitting any lofty goals can spiral you back to the couch.

Next, let's identify the old triggers and programming we need to change. Friends, take a moment and reflect on this because it is very important for your progress.

Write down what it is you keep telling yourself you can't do. Now, rip it up and throw it away. Your business, your body, and your health are all ready for you to take the next steps. This is your kick in the booty to let you know there is no time to waste! Waiting will only delay the results you deserve. There will be no more "I will start on Mondays," NO!!! For the love of Pete, start now!!

Now that you have learned the power of a growth mindset, you can't turn back now from imminent, positive change!

MINDSET Reflection

1. On a scale of 1-10, how is your current *MINDSET* affecting your life?

1 – 2 – 3 – 4 – 5 – 6 – 7 – 8 – 9 – 10

2. Who are the people who have contributed to your *MINDSET*? Who will you choose to help you move forward, and who will you kick to the curb, lol?

3. What is your I DECIDE statement about your *MINDSET*? Write down your power statement below. Get specific!

4. When your *MINDSET* shifts, how do you expect to feel different? Do you feel healthier? Happier? More successful?

5. Where will this decision take you? Envision your life in five years and be specific.

6. Why is your *MINDSET* shift important to you?

~ 2 ~
Excuse Me!!

"A real decision is measured by the fact that you've taken a new action. If there's no action, you haven't truly decided."
- Tony Robbins

We know you've probably read a few books already on breakthrough tips to lead a successful life, and you're still letting yourself accept the excuses. Or maybe you don't even recognize you're making the excuses: I don't have time. I don't have the money. I don't have the skills, support, or discipline. We have said it all, but in this chapter, we will take the "buts" out of it and get this party started for your life.

Don't be fooled. Before we decided to become successful entrepreneurs, we were the ones in the romance section of Barnes & Noble, reading all the Joan Collins and Harlequin novels we could find. We are now glorified personal development junkies and advocates. Put an Ed Mylett podcast in our ears, and we are geeking out on the phone with each other about which part we liked best.

Don't ask us the newest artist on the radio because we would both fail at looking cool. But we can show you some of the best tools we've learned over the years to take action and kick the "buts" and excuses to the door.

According to a study by OnePoll, guess what the most common excuse the average American gives is? Yep, "I am too tired." I think I said it the other day, maybe even yesterday. Who knows? Maybe even this morning. *I'm so tired. I don't know if I can make one more phone call or sit at my computer and get any of those emails out today.* The key is to recognize the difference between *I am too tired* as an excuse, and *I am too tired*, as your body is mentally and physically exhausted. Don't get us wrong. We understand the importance of a good night's sleep, but we have also decided that our dreams and goals for our families are bigger than any excuses. And think about it, what if you keep saying, "I am too tired" to take an extra call, and that one call that you passed up could have changed everything?

According to the poll, the next biggest excuse is, "I don't have enough money." Money, money, money. We'll talk about wealth later, but this is about money standing in the way of your decision to move forward. We've all been there. I'll never forget the feeling of trying to buy a bagel on a Saturday morning, living on my own in Chicago, working my very first job, and getting up to the front of the line after a long wait and my card declining. Ouch! And I can sadly say that this experience did not happen just once. I may have had a bruised ego, but I would not let my empty bank account stand in the way of my dreams of reaching big-city success. Whether it's a bagel or a building purchase, successful people don't let the lack of resources keep them stuck, at least not for long. We learn how to get past it and find a way around it. I don't eat bagels much now—I wonder if that's why? Or maybe I need to eat more of them and revel in my journey.

The third most common excuse for Americans is, "I don't have enough time." Time waits for no one, and we don't want time to get in the way of you and your decisions. Let's be honest. The things we don't make time for are usually the things we might not find important. It sounds better to say we don't have time than it's not important to me right now. We love how

Ed Mylett has taught himself to take the same 24 hours we all have in the day and break it up into six-hour mini-days. His first six-hour day to get work done, emails, and social media. The second part of his mini-day is personal. I bet there's a lot of stuff happening there. And the third part of his mini-day is wrapping up emails, work, etc. The shortened spurts throughout the day not only feel more doable, but we tend to accomplish more in small chunks of time. Genius, right?—we knew those podcast obsessions would come in handy. *I don't have time,* looks a bit different now. What if we helped you make the decision to take the "don't" out of it?

There will never be 25 hours in a day. Think of some of the most successful people in the world. Guess what? They have the same amount of time we do. What if your business was generating $1 million monthly? Would you stop making excuses and find the time to put in more effort, work, and passion? We bet you would say, "Yes!" What if you treated your business as if you were already there? How would that look? Let's commit together not to let any excuse of time stand in our way.

Although these are the three top excuses, we can't ignore the many other ones sprinkled throughout our day that can slow down our progress. Identify each excuse you commonly use and ask yourself, *Why am I trying to get out of doing the work?* We have found that when the desire to do something is so strong, and the decision has been made to do it, the excuses become obsolete. The trouble areas are when you wobble on the desire and decisions, then the excuses flow. What if you had worked months to train for a goal, and then the following happened to you?

As I stood in the crowd of runners at the Chicago Marathon in 2000, I was shivering in running shorts in 30-degree weather. My mind was messing with me. All the awkward feelings of being a gangly, uncoordinated, and too tall at a young age, teenager flooded my brain. I was fighting all the thoughts: *You can't run 26.2 miles. Look at these people around you. They even know that you're an amateur. You're a fraud. You will never make it. You will let your running partner down.* It was brain torture, and I was doing it to myself. From the first day my running partner, Mary, told me that we were going to do a marathon, I doubted my own ability, but her confidence and total conviction that we could and would do this carried me through the entire training process and to this day.

When the gun went off, and the 40,000-person crowd started to move toward the starting line, I teared up. My body was shaking. But a wave of belief that we had made it this far carried me to push out the doubt, lean into my faith and my trusty friend's belief, and to make this happen. We had followed the training to a "T." We bought the books, we had the gear, we had the goop. We had planned for everything except that at the mile six water station, when most runners had warmed up, all of a sudden, countless runners stripped a layer and threw their sweatshirts on the ground. That is when I rolled my left ankle and yelped out a small cry from the sharp pain. At that moment, it happened. I said to my running partner and friend, "Keep going." I thought, *We will not stop for a silly rolled ankle. This will not be my excuse.* So on we went. Our husbands were meeting us with our cheering kids on as many corners as they could get to, and three and a half hours later, my ankle was the size of King Kong's ankle. It had me jogging so slowly, and I begged my partner to run on without me. But I wasn't going to stop.

I just needed to go at my own slow pace to finish. In 4 hours and 23 minutes, I crossed the line crying like a baby. They were big happy tears. It was a top ten day in my life. They had to cut my shoe off, but I was so happy I never felt the pain. No excuses were going to stop me that day. We had planned for it all, except an injury. But by forcing out the negative, I decided that day was my day to do what seemed impossible to me. At one point, all the teenage angst and bad memories were pushed out and replaced with positive, hopeful determination. So, friends, what do you keep telling yourself you can't do? Time to unlock it and throw it away. It may be time for me to run another marathon with two good ankles.

> *"Get your mind going in the right direction, and you'll get your life going in the right direction." - Joel Osteen.*

One of the first parts of letting go of excuses is to understand the power of words you speak into the world and yourself because they truly matter. For example, do we say we want to eat healthy when someone offers us something we shouldn't be eating, like a dessert? Then we instantly change our stance, act weak, and say, "Oh, I can't have that. Poor me." Or do we own our position and decision and say, "Thanks, but I am choosing not to eat dessert these days to hit a goal, and I am psyched to make it happen."

The language we use around our decision is key. The power and resilience will come from our own strength in words. If you act and speak like what you are trying to accomplish is too hard or impossible to sustain, then you will begin to believe it, and the people around you will also see that it won't last. If we had the power right now, we would command you to change your words. Be conscious of what you say in your head and to others. Trust us, if you tell enough people you are weak long enough, then they will start to believe you. But on the contrary, if you tell them you are a strong, badass winner long enough, they will believe that too. We decide, not them.

Say it with us now, friends: *I decide. I decide. I decide.*

There is something called an excuse cycle. That is when you make an important life decision and make a plan to succeed in one area of your life that needs change, but in the process, other areas of your life are slipping or possibly failing. For example, let's say you are kicking booty on your new budget or rocking your new healthier lifestyle. But then you start to notice other areas of your life slipping, which ultimately defeats the purpose of the greatness you started with your new direction and decision. Our good friend Tony shared his story about quitting drinking, and he's now twelve years sober. This is so massive! We are proud of him for his sobriety and his soaring business! Still, he surprisingly shared that he caught himself succumbing to bad eating habits because, in his brain, he was thinking, *Since I'm doing so well in this area, not drinking, it's okay to cheat in other areas like my eating habits.*

He quickly tightened up his eating. He cleaned up his diet, which gave him an even greater sense of accomplishment by getting back on track. His ability to recognize this took him out of the excuse cycle and put him on a straighter path to success in other areas.

The hardest thing to swallow is that bad excuses will ultimately hurt you and slow your journey down—no one else. The self-deception and ultimate self-sabotage is not following through and ends up a solid pain point in your life, becoming a weight to carry. You have the personal ability to stop the pattern and rewrite your programming, just like Tony did. It's time to understand our own personal patterns, including an "excuse dialogue": *What do you tell yourself? What do others tell you? And what have you been told that is affecting your results?*

A tracking method, at the end of the day, will show you what you've done and maybe what you haven't done. It can be that simple. Let's take it one step further. Did you know if you show your tracking to someone else, it's 76% more likely you will accomplish your daily tasks? Who will that person be for you?

I excuse, you excuse, we all excuse. NO MORE!!!

What if you start with a "no excuse day," then move to a "no excuse weekend," then a "no excuse month." Can you imagine the progress you would see if you gave zero excuses and did the work for a solid month? Doing this can ultimately reset habits and provide glorious results. Go, sis!

We believe in you. Talk about some insane excuses! How about the number one excuse? Your health. Let's dive in!

EXCUSES Reflection

1. On a scale of 1-10, how are your current *EXCUSES* affecting your life?

1 - 2 - 3 - 4 - 5 - 6 - 7 - 8 - 9 - 10

2. Who are the people who have contributed to your *EXCUSES*? Who will you choose to help you move forward, and who will you kick to the curb, lol?

3. What is your IDECIDE statement about your *EXCUSES*?

Write down your power statement below. Get specific!

4. When your *EXCUSES* shift, how do you expect to feel different? Do you feel healthier? Happier? More successful?

5. Where will this decision take you? Envision your life in five years and be specific.

6. Why is your *EXCUSES* shift important to you?

~ 3 ~
Weight for it!

*"I say if I'm beautiful, I say if I'm strong.
You will not determine my story. I will."*
- **Amy Schumer**

Remember when healthy eating was a plain bagel and a Diet Coke? Times have changed, and so has the knowledge and research which shows us how to better care for our bodies. But what if you had the power to make healthy decisions and choices for yourself because you really *want* to, not because you *have* to? Our daily choices ultimately affect the long-term outcome. The "I choose not to eat sugar" rather than "I can't have sugar" can be the difference in a successful health journey.

Healthline magazine says self-talk is something you do naturally throughout your waking hours. People are becoming more aware that positive self-talk is a powerful tool for increasing self-confidence and curbing negative emotions. People who can master positive self-talk are thought to be more confident, motivated and productive. Our beloved Brené Brown, professor at the University of Houston Graduate College and motivational speaker, refers to the negative self-talk in her head as the "gremlins." By giving her negative thoughts names, she steps away from them and pokes fun at them. Humor always seems to win. In our quest for healthier bodies and lives, we must stay intentional with our words. One of those words we often hear and struggle with is "dieting."

Okay, how long have you been on the roller coaster of dieting? Let's get off that ride together. Both of us are raising daughters and are very conscious about the "D-word" and why dieting is temporary. Instead of dieting, we want to create healthier lifestyles that last. We have always been conscious of our words and choices around our girls. What they see and hear will ultimately affect them when they are older. Let's not mistake what we are saying. We want nothing more than for you to be healthy in your life. That doesn't have to mean what size pants you are currently wearing, but the habits you are putting into your daily life to get one step closer to a healthy body, mind and soul. We all have access at our fingertips to nutritional information and research. But it is what we do with that information that can be slow to follow.

We have the opportunity to help men and women every day take their health back into their own hands. We have found that a deeper dive into their past will lead us to the source of their unhealthy habits. Maybe you were raised in a family that didn't have a healthy lifestyle. Guess what? That's okay. But the big question is, are you going to break the cycle for yourself or for your family? Being healthy is, most times, gaining the tools and knowledge to put healthy habits into play. We beg you to change your old programming and turn to a new station. It stops here, and it stops with you. Making that choice sometimes doesn't come easy. Sometimes it's taking a hard look in the mirror, literally, as our friend Lisa M. shares.

My turning point was when I stepped on the scale, and the number looking back at me was very close to when I was nine months pregnant. But this time, I was not pregnant. I can honestly say I was fearful that this was going to be my "new normal." And I know that some people would have simply accepted it. I waited for 45 years to find an incredible man who I loved so much. And more than anything, I wanted to be comfortable in my own skin with him. One night, I finally opened up and told him that my weight made me feel self-conscious and uncomfortable being naked in front of him. That was hard to admit, but it was the truth. It was my truth. And he told me he already knew. He candidly told me that he thinks I'm beautiful and sexy, exactly how I am, but what matters is how I see myself. And he wanted me to be confident and comfortable with him, whether I was naked or clothed and that our connection mattered. In that moment, I knew I was done with this. It wasn't me.

After that conversation, I looked in the mirror and was reminded I was always a strong, confident, imperfect woman. And it was time for me to get back to that. The question was, how was I going to do it? I was overwhelmed with how to take this weight off, and I resorted to getting two consultations for a tummy tuck. This was going to be major surgery, a six-week recovery period, and tens of thousands of dollars I was willing to spend because I was that overwhelmed with my new reality. But the truth was, I was using it as an "easy way out." I wouldn't have to do the work if someone cut the fat off. The first doctor told me he would do it, but I wasn't happy with the consult and continued my search for a doctor that made me feel more comfortable and was more willing to answer my extensive questions. I researched online for days. I came across a plastic surgeon from Orlando, Florida, and I was convinced that this was the doctor for me. His work was beautiful, but his prices were 50% higher—I didn't care.

So after sending several close-up naked photos of my stomach, sides and back, it was finally time for my video consultation. That morning, the doctor gave me the most humbling news. He said I wasn't a candidate for a tummy tuck. He informed me that the purpose of a tummy tuck was to remove the loose skin after weight loss, not to remove the fat itself. He told me to schedule another consultation after I lost approximately 15 to 20 pounds of fat, and then I would be a better candidate. He also explained that I carried visceral fat, the fat that surrounds your organs—you know, the most dangerous kind. I thanked him for his honesty and professionalism, disconnected from the video, and cried. I was overwhelmed. I was humiliated and very disappointed in myself.

The thought of calling my new husband to share this embarrassment of a consultation made me want to crawl into a hole. I picked up the phone and called him at work. I shared the consultation results and promised him I would lose the weight. He had already lost one wife to cancer. I was not going to put him through another wife having unnecessary health issues due to visceral fat. He listened quietly and promised to support me no matter what. And then we decided we could do this together. And we did.

Twenty pounds lighter, I looked at my loose skin, and I knew I was now a perfect candidate. And you know what? I didn't do it because I originally wanted to do it for the wrong reasons. I was using it as a means of weight loss. I didn't have to do the hard work because I didn't know how to do the hard work. But I decided to figure it out, make it happen, and look and feel healthier for myself and my new husband. This worked out exactly the way it was supposed to, and I couldn't be more grateful.

How bad does it have to get before it's time to dig deep? Do you have to hear, like Lisa did, that it is the bad fat that can ultimately shorten your lifespan? This can be a tall and treacherous mountain for many of us, but we want to take it one step at a time, one day at a time, and one choice at a time.

Have you seen or do you love the show *The Home Edit*? I know we do in our households. Not only because they are hysterical and cute but because they have given us a different way of looking at the organization of food. In this case, they give viewers a practical, fun way to look at the food staring at us on the pantry shelf in the "healthy green category." They suggest it be front and center and to put the "not so healthy" foods on the higher shelf so we can't see them in those snack bins. Talk about reverse psychology at its best!

Another example of reverse psychology we love to use and coach has to do with fashion. We may not have research to back this up, but we definitely fall into the "dress the part" of being healthy. Buy yourself that cute workout set that gives you a bit of a pep in your step to get out of the house. Don't initially buy the outfit size for when you hit your goals. Instead, buy the ones that fit you now, that will motivate you, and you will stand taller today. You deserve it.

The definition of "health," according to the Merriam-Webster Dictionary: *the condition of being sound in body, mind and spirit, or a condition in which someone or something is thriving or doing well.* Friends, it's not just about the outside but also about the inside. Our health can send us back to our mindset in chapter one, but it also starts deep down in our spirit. We thought it would be fun to share some of our daily practices that have helped us along the way.

1. *Meal planning.* We're no Giada! Jump on Pinterest and grab some family-friendly recipes to plan for the week ahead. By following a healthy meal plan, it will not only ensure you're eating the right foods at the right times, but it will also keep you on budget and save you time. Benjamin Franklin famously said, "If you fail to plan, you plan to fail."

2. *Scheduling your workouts.* We never seem to miss that doctor's appointment scheduled months in advance. Why are we not scheduling our workouts, so they become a part of our daily life?

3. *Time Blocking.* Time blocking has been a game changer for us in our business and health. Taking the time to block out small amounts of time throughout your day allows you to get so much more done and make room for your scheduled workouts and self-care.

4. *Start your day strong.* One of the most successful daily practices is an early morning routine and how you start your day. A great example we continue to use in our morning routines is illustrated in a book called *Miracle Morning* by Hal Elrod.

Miracle Morning gives you a wonderful outline and example of how to etch your morning routine in stone. Basically, if you need to wake up a little earlier than normal to get things done, then you do that. You plan some quiet time, maybe without your children awake or your husband or wife wanting breakfast. Whatever it is, you have to be the one that wakes up and gives yourself this time. During this time, you're going to set your morning by getting yourself in this wonderful peaceful zone where you put yourself first. You have a little bit of quiet time. Maybe it's for meditation or prayer. You read some pages out of a positive book. Maybe it's a network marketing book, an influential book, maybe it's the Bible, or maybe it's just an uplifting book that makes you feel good for that day. And then, you take some extra time to say your gratitudes out loud. It's hard to be stressed and upset when you have a grateful mind and grateful words are coming out of your mouth.

The morning is a wonderful time to get some exercise, 20 minutes or just a few sit-ups, to get your body moving. Then, when you turn to your family for the rest of your day, you are calm and centered and have set yourself up for success.

The next step is simply to breathe. This is one of the most important components of our day. We have found that many of us never take a full breath during our day. Start your breathing early—take some full breaths in, and breathe out.

5. *Hydration.* Fill your water jug so that you are drinking tons of water throughout your day. Water consumption helps maximize physical and mental performance to keep you at your absolute best.

6. *Intentionality.* One of our daily practices is putting our phones down, having intentional time with the people we love, and building relationships. Sometimes we have to put our phones in another room in the house so that we are not distracted. This is especially important these days with so many working from home.

7. *Focus.* You need to learn to have focus throughout your day. Many people attempt to multitask, but studies show (Dr. Travis Bradberry, "Why Smart People Don't Multitask") it kills performance and may even damage your brain. Every time we multitask, we are not just harming our performance in that moment but an area in our brain that is critical to our future success. Working on your focus is another daily practice that will change the way and the results you're trying to achieve within your day.

6. *Visualization.* This has been key to helping us in our business. If you could see our offices, they are filled with sticky notes with positive words of affirmation such as, *I am worthy. I am capable. I am deserving.* Those pieces of paper are not only giving us visuals of what we're working towards but also a continued belief of what we are doing and where we're headed. If you cannot see clearly what it is you're working for, my friends, start with visualization to see where your road is taking you.

7. *Personal development.* Not a day goes by that we don't start our day with prayer, positivity, and personal development. A minimum of ten minutes a day can change everything. Personal development can be a podcast or a book, it can be anything that fills your spirit, fills your soul, and gives you the tools to start your day in a motivated, positive way.

8. *Checklists.* Things don't always get done the way we had intended. There's something about taking out a pen and paper and not only writing the tasks we plan to achieve but crossing off what we accomplished during the day. At the end of every day, we do a review and make our list of the "top threes." These are the three things that did not get accomplished today but will be top priorities for the next morning.

9. *Beauty sleep.* You are talking to two ladies who love their sleep. There is something more to just getting sleep—it is resetting our minds and resetting our brains. It gives us the energy and focus to wake up the next day energized and grateful. Beauty sleep is your friend.

10. *Journaling.* Journaling yields incredible benefits for your mental and physical health. If you're like many of us, your journal is

collecting dust in the back of your desk drawer. But countless studies show that journaling is a powerful way to boost our mental health, reduce depression and anxiety, and make us happier and more content with our lives.

Hopefully, this gives you plenty of tools for your health marathon. These tools for making better daily choices will be small, positive steps to the overall results. Are you reading this and feeling overwhelmed? You could just pick one tool at a time that stood out to you and start there. Your health and body will thank you.

HEALTH Reflection

1. On a scale of 1-10, how is your current *HEALTH* affecting your life?

    1 - 2 - 3 - 4 - 5 - 6 - 7 - 8 - 9 - 10

2. Who are the people who have contributed to your *HEALTH*? Who will you choose to help you move forward, and who will you kick to the curb, lol?

3. What is your I DECIDE statement about your *HEALTH*?

    Write down your power statement below. Get specific!

4. When your *HEALTH* shifts, how do you expect to feel different? Do you feel healthier? Happier? More successful?

5. Where will this decision take you? Envision your life in five years and be specific.

6. Why is your *HEALTH* shift important to you?

~ 4 ~
Mo Money Honey!

"The only difference between a rich person and a poor person is how they use their time."
- Robert Kiyosaki

We commonly hear the adage that money buys happiness and money makes the world go around, which suggests that money is highly significant. It is the most important or one of the most important things in life to people. But that same money causes wars and is the number one stressor in most relationships, and it separates people in our society.

Knowing the massive gap between having or not having money can make a huge difference in life. Are you the consummate saver who saves all your money for a rainy day? Or are you an overspender who has more "month" than money? It is important to look at your relationship with money and how it is influenced by your past life experiences and decisions. Can you identify a person or timeline that shaped your money habits?

My amazing sister Shannon has opened our eyes to our relationship with money. Here is her story.

I was driving on the 405 freeway in Los Angeles, and if you know the 405, you know it can give you lots of time to think.

I was 26 years old and had just been named the top performer in the company, winning an all-expense two-week trip to Australia and New Zealand. You would think I would be screaming, singing my favorite song. But instead, all I could think was, "Is this it?" I had my job wired and was not challenged. My dream was to be a financial adviser, focusing on the behavioral side of finance. I had taken a significant paying sales role with a financial company and got comfortable. At that moment, I knew no one was coming to rescue me by tapping me on the shoulder and giving me my dream career. I had to go back to an entry-level position, not making a lot of money, and back to school for a graduate degree.

After returning from Australia and New Zealand, I tendered my resignation and started on my journey to be the financial professional I hoped to be. They were the most challenging and rewarding years of my life. Thirty years later, I have built a very successful financial planning practice and financial literacy business. And last year, I was honored to be asked to do a Ted Talk.

For almost three decades now, I have had a front-row seat to the financial lives of hundreds of individuals and families. I don't just write a report about financial literacy, I live it with real people daily. And what I've learned is that money is emotional. We all know that. But for some reason, when it comes to money, we believe that we should be logical and think we can make rational decisions around our money and investments without our emotions influencing those decisions.

Unfortunately, my experience is that that is not the case because we all think we should be logical. An enormous amount of shame comes with a lack of financial knowledge. Suppose you opened your computer right now and searched for a financial literacy topic. You would find hundreds, if not thousands, of articles and websites where you can find information on any economic issue. With all this readily available information, why is money consistently ranked as one of the top stressors? I believe it's because our emotions, past wounds, and experiences with money impact our ability to make sound financial decisions, and we don't even recognize them.

I call it "financial scar tissue," which may keep you from achieving financial satisfaction and happiness. Financial scar tissue is a habit, memory, or action around money that can hurt you or cause you emotional pain. Take a moment and think about your relationship with money. Do you have money habits or memories resulting from your experience? How are those experiences impacting how you handle or feel about money now? Are your experiences and memories supporting a healthy, happy relationship with money? Or are they keeping you from money satisfaction?

Most people think that more money would solve all their problems. I'm afraid I have to disagree. When we learn to align our resources with our values, we find financial success at all levels of wealth—aligning your money with your values.

At 13, my father and I were taking a walk in our neighborhood after dinner. The sun was starting to set, and we ran into our neighbor who was building a new home that was the largest I had ever seen. I had not met the neighbor yet, but my dad seemed to know him and stood discussing with him the new home that was at least three times the size of our house. For a long time, I remember being bored and frustrated with the length of the conversation. My mind drifted, and I started to examine the man's shoes. He wore plain white tennis shoes, not any recognizable brand, and they had green mold all around the edges; it appeared to be growing on the shoes. At

13, I was baffled that this man building a massive home on our block would have mold on his shoes. Now, shoes are often a big deal to a 13-year-old girl, and I was no exception. Once my dad had finished the conversation, we continued our walk. I was full of questions about this man with the mold on his shoes.

"If he was so rich building this huge home, why did he not buy a new pair of shoes?" I asked my dad.

My father's answer was simple but deeply profound. The shoes fill his needs, and he does not care what you or anyone else thinks about them. My dad talked about how you can find true wealth by aligning your money and values with what is important to you, not what others think.

I would love to tell you that I fully understood what he meant at the time. But it took years of working with clients one on one for me to appreciate his wisdom.

You can find true wealth when you align your money with your values.

I had forgotten the moldy shoes entirely until one day, early in my career as a financial advisor, I sat across from a couple telling me how badly they wanted to travel. They had just purchased a home. After their new mortgage payment, insurance and taxes, they had very little money left monthly to travel. I asked them why they bought the house at the cost of traveling. They told me they felt it was their next step, the right thing to do. After further conversation, it became apparent that their parents had pressured them to buy a home, and they had extended themselves a bit as their incomes grew. They were in their early 30s, newly married, and had been renting. They were working professionals with no kids. They had envisioned themselves traveling on their vacations to exotic destinations, but the home purchase had drained their cash reserve. They could not travel and were experiencing so much pressure with a huge mortgage that they felt stuck in their jobs.

They were not happy financially. During the 90s, a term often used for this was "house poor." And this young couple felt the "house poor" pressure. That is when I remembered the mold and took the conversation in a different direction. For the first time, I asked them, "If you can align your money with what you value most, what would it look like?" The room fell silent, and it was difficult for them to answer. There was such an overwhelming sense of responsibility around doing what made them look successful to the outside world (owning a home) that they were sacrificing their happiness and did not even know why. We continued the conversation about what they would want their lives to look like if they had the money to travel, and they lit up. The home was not only preventing them from traveling, but it also locked them in jobs they didn't love or had room to grow in. They were miserable. That is when I told them to sell the house. They were stunned for a moment. Then the excitement in their voices grew as they thought about living life on their terms, with their priorities. Just because you make a financial decision, you are not always beholden to that decision for the rest of your life.

There are many decisions that you choose to reverse or not pursue any further. I like the example of a home because it is a large purchase that feels permanent. It is not as impactful when we make a small financial decision that is out of alignment with our values. But a home will be one of the most significant purchases of our lives. If we feel like we made a mistake and feel too strapped financially or are just not happy, we tend to gut it out. Why? Because society tells us that specific financial accomplishments define our success. And home ownership, at least here in the USA, is one of the critical measures of a young person's success. Society's expectations around money, home ownership, and getting the right job to support a lifestyle have added *to our emotional and financial scar tissue and trauma. Social media has created an online currency of likes, influencers and curated imagery. How is it impacting our lives? Is it influencing the financial decisions we make? What is most important to you financially? Are you living in alignment with your values and desires around money? One of the hardest lessons to learn is determining what is important to you financially, not your family, friends, or Instagram.*

Ultimately, being financially happy is getting what we want. Many think we are financially striving for what we want but are trying to please someone else's parents, friends, or social media. Our society is all about "looking good for the picture" for just that particular moment in time. It portrays financial satisfaction but actually we need to find incredible financial happiness that is within our income boundaries where we are aligning our money with our values.

With those amazing stories and life examples, we also need to know that a huge part of being where you want to be financially is overcoming the shame of wanting more. The only person who can create that shame is you in your own head with negative self-talk or memories from past experiences of someone trying to drag you down with them instead of celebrating your success. It's like crabs in a bucket. When you put a bunch of crabs in a bucket, and one tries to climb out, the others pull that one back into the bucket before it escapes, keeping them all on the same level. Do not let the opinions of others about your finances or wealth get you pulled down into the bucket of crabs.

Let's face it, our thoughts and feelings around money can be unhealthy. But we still all need it. It creates security, and we need to embrace the inner child that was told money doesn't buy happiness. We need to realize that it may not buy "happy," but it does provide comfort, a roof over our heads, and sometimes an outfit or two that makes us feel some joy. So decide to be smart, decide your why, and embrace the hard work to achieve the financial goals that match your values, needs, and wants.

Listen, friends, the best lesson anyone has ever taught us is to keep going. *Do not put a timestamp on your financial success.* We have already heard twice in this book two very successful women sharing that no one is coming to rescue them, spurring them on to rescue themselves. This self-saving attitude will serve you well in life.

I was the middle child of three sisters, and believe me, dad wanted a boy so badly and got three girls. He raised us strong and taught us to do everything a boy could do. He gave us constant and annoying lectures on how we could rule the world, make as much money as we wanted, serve others and run companies. Even in the early 70s, he taught us to stand up for ourselves and not wait for someone else to give us the life we wanted. All of those fireside chats and lectures sunk in, and we are all now independent leaders in our industries. But more importantly, when we want something or want to contribute to the world, we know that it is up to us to decide and make it happen.

It is a gift that you can give yourself. And if you want more money, wealth, or even to tithe more at church, keep going until you get it. Dean Graziosi says it best, "You always hear that money doesn't buy happiness. You obviously haven't given enough away." We give you permission to decide and seek your financial dreams with no shame for wanting more.

FINANCES Reflection

1. On a scale of 1-10, how are your current *FINANCES* affecting your life?

1 - 2 - 3 - 4 - 5 - 6 - 7 - 8 - 9 - 10

2. Who are the people who have contributed to your *FINANCES*? Who will you choose to help you move forward, and who will you kick to the curb, lol?

3. What is your I DECIDE statement about your *FINANCES*?

Write down your power statement below. Get specific!

4. When your *FINANCES* shift, how do you expect to feel different? Do you feel healthier? Happier? More successful?

5. Where will this decision take you? Envision your life in five years and be specific.

6. Why are your *FINANCES important* to you?

~ 5 ~
Say Cheese!

"Be happy, be bright, be you"
- **Kate Spade**

When we are surrounded by perfectly poised and edited photos on social media, we find it harder than ever to feel good about ourselves. It is nearly impossible not to compare your life to others when staring back at what looks like perfection. "Comparitis" kills! What if we decided to allow ourselves to embrace the journey and finally let go? Do you find yourself growing, changing, succeeding, and not finding your emotions of happiness aligning with your journey? That may be the overall point. Life will not always be filled with the emotion of feeling happy, but accepting the ups and downs and embracing that you are alive and breathing. When we can decide to adapt to the roller coaster of life, we are unlocking the doors to the potential beyond our wildest dreams. Basically, friends, don't let the fake make you frown.

We've seen an uptick in mental health problems in the past few years. I remember vividly sitting on the couch with my girls, watching a much-anticipated performance of Simone Biles at the 2021 Olympics. As she huddled with her coach, they quickly announced she would not be competing. The world went crazy. How could the top gymnast in the world be walking away from what she could probably perform in her sleep? I remember my daughter looking up at me and saying, "She doesn't look happy." Plain and simple. She has the talent, the knowledge and the skills, but her mental health was affected, and she knew at that moment she had to make the decision to walk away. This is a recent and dramatic example that brought mental health to the forefront of our society.

One important thing to remember is that happiness isn't a state of constant euphoria. Instead, happiness is an overall sense of experiencing more positive emotions than negative emotions. Happiness is such a broadly defined term. Psychologists and other social scientists typically use the term "subject well-being." When they talk about this emotional state, just as it sounds, "subject well-being" tends to focus on individuals' overall personal feelings about their life in the present.

Two key components of happiness or "subject well-being" are, *first*, the balance of emotions: everyone experiences both positive and negative emotions, feelings and moods. Happiness is genuinely linked to experiencing more positive feelings than negative ones. And *second* is life satisfaction. This relates to how satisfied you feel with different areas of your life, including your relationships, work, achievements and other things that you consider important.

Another definition of happiness comes from the ancient philosopher Aristotle, who suggested that happiness is the one human desire and all other human desires exist as a way to obtain happiness. He believed there were four levels of happiness: immediate gratification, comparison and achievement, making positive contributions, and achieving fulfillment. Happiness, Aristotle suggested, could be achieved through the golden mean, which involves finding a balance between deficiency and excess.

Here are some signs of happiness. While perceptions of happiness may be different from one person to the next, there are some key indicators that psychologists look for when measuring and assessing happiness. Key signs include:

- feeling like you're living the life you wanted.
- Going with the flow and a willingness to take life as it comes.
- Feeling that the conditions of your life are good.
- Enjoying positive.
- Healthy relationships with other people.
- Feeling that you have accomplished or will accomplish what you want in life.
- Feeling satisfied with your current life.
- Feeling positive more than negative.
- Being open to new ideas and experiences.
- Practicing self-care and treating yourself with kindness and compassion.
- Experiencing gratitude.
- Feeling that you are living life with a sense of meaning and purpose.
- Wanting to share your happiness and joy with others.

Happy people still feel the whole range of human emotions: anger, frustration, boredom, loneliness and even sadness from time to time. But even when faced with discomfort, they have an underlying sense of optimism that things will get better, that they can deal with what is happening, and that they can feel happy again.

The Benefits of Optimism

Different types of happiness play an important role in the overall experience. Some may be pleasurable, while others might skew one way or the other. Have you ever volunteered for a cause you believe in that gave you a sense of meaning rather than pleasure? Watching your favorite TV show, on the other hand, might rank lower in meaning and higher in pleasure. Here are some types of happiness that we hope you can identify with in your own life:

- *Joy* - Joy is often a relatively fleeting feeling in the present moment.

- *Excitement* - A happy feeling that involves looking forward to something with positive anticipation.

- *Gratitude* - A positive emotion that involves being thankful and appreciative.

- *Pride* - A feeling of satisfaction and something that you have accomplished.

- *Optimism* - A way of looking at life with a positive, upbeat outlook.

- *Contentment* - This type of happiness involves a sense of satisfaction.

> **Say it with us:** *I decide to be happy and grateful and have a positive mindset on the journey of life. I will embrace and identify the different types of happiness in all areas. I understand and accept life's darker moments and do not see them as negative setbacks. But when the pendulum of life goes down, we will choose to come back up.*

How do you walk through your day? Friends, when you really think about your attitude and how you wear your emotions on your sleeve, what does your day look like? What is your happy level each day? We were fortunate to have my husband's mother live to the wonderful age of 97. And something very important that she taught us about happiness and sharing happiness with others came from her little outings. At 97, she would drive herself to the store just to walk around, not needing to purchase anything. But because she lived alone in an assisted care facility, sometimes those little outings were the brightest parts of her day. She would share with us that sometimes she would walk up and down the aisles and just look into people's faces, and they looked like zombies. They wouldn't look up, they wouldn't smile, and they certainly wouldn't say hello. And whenever she did see someone that would catch her eye, she would say, "Hi, how are you today?" She was so friendly and brought joy into their world that most of the time, if she could catch their attention, they would return the pleasantries, which would make her day.

So how do you walk through your day? Is your head down? Are you not looking at other people or saying hello? It reminds us of Dolly Parton. She always says, "If you see someone without a smile, give them yours." If we could raise our happiness levels by giving "happy" to other people throughout our day, it would certainly raise how we feel. Okay, let's reset. Breathe in, breathe out, smile and let's choose happiness.

HAPPINESS Reflection

1. On a scale of 1-10, how is your current *state of HAPPINESS* affecting your life?

1 - 2 - 3 - 4 - 5 - 6 - 7 - 8 - 9 - 10

2. Who are the people who have contributed to your *HAPPINESS*? Who will you choose to help you move forward, and who will you kick to the curb, lol?

3. What is your I DECIDE statement about your *HAPPINESS*?

Write down your power statement below. Get specific!

4. When your *HAPPINESS* shifts, how do you expect to feel different? Do you feel healthier? More successful? Grateful?

5. Where will this decision take you? Envision your life in five years and be specific.

6. Why is your *happiness* shift important to you?

~ 6 ~
Get Outta My Way!

*"If you believe it will work out, you will see opportunities.
If you believe it won't, you will see obstacles."*
- Wayne Dyer

What doesn't kill us makes us stronger. But friends, we are not here to ignore the struggles and challenges. We're here to help you decide to work through it, keep going and embrace the entire journey. Let's admit that actually embracing the hard times is one of the hardest and most uncomfortable things to do. But it is in the discomfort where we dig deep and work harder to build ourselves up. Similar to a bodybuilder who, to grow their muscles, has to push past their comfort level and cause trauma to the muscle fibers, referred to as actual muscle injury or damage. In essence, the body's repair begins and increases muscle strength and size, similar to the challenges we face in life. We have experienced so many times when a team member will come to us for support, and they are feeling so challenged and down that the tears start flowing, and I see it immediately as a good thing. *Tears?* Yes, tears are not bad. Tears show frustration or sadness but also passion and represent a point where people are ready to draw that line in the sand and move forward—it's a turning point.

Challenges take us to the brink. And guess what? The brink is where it all happens. The brink is where you feel in your soul that you want change, that you want more, that you need more, and will do what it takes to seek just that.

This is the story of our friend Michelle. Talk about taking you to the brink and back.

I will never forget this one Saturday. I lied to my husband, telling him that I wanted to clean out my closet. But the real reason was our closet had a window to the front of our house that I had spent the entire afternoon looking out, waiting for the FedEx truck to arrive with my prescription pills so that I could get to them before my husband did. I have tears streaming down my face right now, remembering that day and still feeling that moment every time I see a FedEx truck.

I had the perfect life. I grew up in a beautiful Christian home with two loving parents. I went to college, married a great man, had two beautiful children and ran a successful Pilates business. This was not the face of a woman hiding an opiate addiction. But here I was, probably two years into a full-blown addiction, and I was hiding in my beautiful master closet, living a lie and waiting desperately for my pills to arrive. I remember my daughter was almost three when she came in asking me to play with her.

I told her, "Mommy is busy. Go play with daddy." When she walked out of the closet, I fell to the floor crying because I had made myself a prisoner of my own reality. And it was a nightmare. How did I get here? How did I let this get this bad? I thought I had control. That was by far one of the most painful moments of my life. I decided right then and there I had to change. I knew the entire time throughout my years of addiction that what I was doing was wrong. But you make up so many excuses in your head to rationalize your behavior. So many people will have a glass of wine at night. So I told myself that popping a few pills after 5:00 p.m. was just my way of relaxing. I justified it for years. It wasn't until I tried to stop the first time that I realized how far into it I was. I tried multiple times to quit on my own, but the withdrawals and the feeling of emptiness were so painful that I would always find myself right back on them.

It was Sunday night, after the closet cleaning incident, when I was at church during worship music, and there was a moment in the song, I Am Redeemed. It tells you to lift your head to look at Jesus when he can make you new. I knew that my story was not over, and with the help of Jesus, I could recover and be the daughter he had created me to be. I felt so scared and so alone. But I knew the only way to recovery was to come clean to my loved ones, get serious about being sober, and lean into him every step of the way. My mindset shifted from thinking I could do it on my own to realizing that I needed major help and couldn't act like I was in control any longer.

After years of hard work, I'm proud to say I'm seven years sober. My marriage is thriving. I have two amazing children and now run two successful businesses. My life has never felt more fulfilled or full of purpose. My life sober is better in every aspect, and I'm on fire to share my story with the world.

It took me five years of sobriety to finally gain the courage to share my story publicly. I had found myself five years into my journey when I started my online business and was sharing my life on social media, but I was hiding such a big part of my story. Mentors and people I had looked up to kept telling me I would know when the time was right if I ever was to listen to that voice inside me. I had been thinking about telling my story for a while and talking to God about it. And one spring morning at my studio, it hit me that I was finally ready. I realized that I had what seemed like a perfect life and went through such a deep, dark and lonely time. There had to be hundreds, if not thousands, of others suffering in silence, just waiting for a hand to reach out to them. I decided no matter how uncomfortable it was to share my story, if it helped just one person, I couldn't ask for more. I was scared of what people would think. I was frightened that my students, who had been taking my classes for years, would continue once they knew my truth.

I had so many doubts when I put out the first video sharing my story, but the outpour of love that came to me was so overwhelming and brought me to tears. I have met so many amazing people, and I personally made connections and helped others in their sobriety journey. My heart will never be more full. I feel my journey is to share my story with as many people as possible and be the light of Christ for those struggling with any addiction. I want to share with everyone that no matter how bad your situation seems, absolutely how low you can get, there is always a way out, and you are the author of your own story. Don't let anyone else write the ending for you.

Michelle's journey is the perfect example of someone who decides to choose not only to walk through it but to work through it. The journey may not always feel good. It may be messy and filled with fear, doubt and instability, but the daily journey will bring us to progress on the other side.

In fact, all progress is winning. The Merriam-Webster dictionary defines progress as this: *a royal journey marked by pomp and pageant, a forward or onward movement and gradual betterment.* So if progress is the "win," each step forward on your journey should be celebrated because it means you are not standing still or sliding backward. Train your brain to be proud of any type of progress. Progress will come in many forms. Progress might be leaning into a new skill to enhance your journey. It could also be as simple as feeling the inner strength to keep going one more day.

Our girlfriend, Bre, shares her journey and where she got the strength to keep going.

2014 was the best and the worst year of my life. It was one of the best when I had my first baby. I've never experienced anything better than becoming a mother to his perfect tiny human. However, 2014 was also one of the worst years of my life when my world was devastated. My father had just passed away, and shortly after, my life was ripped apart because of my husband's sex addiction. I unexpectedly found myself a single mom.

I was struggling with my career, anxiety, shame, depression, and the list goes on. I was completely broken. I sold my house and moved in with my family for emotional support. I was pretending I was fine when I was really crumbling inside. I would act like I was put together and that I could do it all, but most days, I didn't want to get out of bed. There was an entire year that I barely left the house except to go to the grocery store. Even then, I remember some days when I would sit and cry in the parking lot because I was too ashamed to go in. My situation worsened because my business relied heavily on working with others. I've always loved marketing and sales, but I suddenly wondered, "How can I be in a people business when I don't want to be around people? I was scraping by in life, and I didn't know how to find a way out. So how did I turn it around? Not very easily. I wish I could tell you I did it overnight, but it took a lot of work.

I envy the people in this world who are born positive, happy, and hardwired for success. Not me. I have to work hard for it. If you were to ask if the glass was half full or half empty, I would probably be thinking, "I don't even like that glass. Who cares what's in it?" I have to fight every single day to focus on gratitude and the good in the world. If I don't, weeds start to grow in my mind. I decided to rely heavily on personal development to grow my mindset and also to fill my daily cups. My faith, which had never been tested like this before, suddenly became my rock.

Receiving therapy and letting professionals help make sense of my situation became my new normal. I turned off the news and took breaks from social media which was filling my head with uncertainty. And finally, I not only forced myself out of bed, but I exercised and moved my body to clear my head to become a stronger version of myself. Even though those were some of the darkest days of my life, I have no regrets. Let me be clear: I never want to go through it again, but I don't regret it. Remember, problems are gifts. If you can survive the pain, you will be introduced to your true self on the other side.

These stories melt our hearts and inspire our souls. Always know deep down that you will and can survive anything and shine brighter on the other side.

- *Keep your eyes on the prize, the goal, the dream, and why you started.*
- *Never forget what brought you to the starting line and got your engine revved up.*
- *Set yourself up for success by filling your surroundings with the right positive influences.*
- *Always look for people who can inspire you, motivate you and help you through any challenge you face.*
- *Surround yourself with mentors and people who encourage and support you to take the next steps through your challenges.*

Obstacles are opportunities, friends. You are strong enough to handle every challenge, wise enough to find a solution, and capable enough to do whatever needs to be done. Every step, every hurdle counts. We see you. We love you, and we believe in you. Look fear in the face and gain the courage, the strength and the confidence to kick that challenge to the curb.

OBSTACLES Reflection

1. On a scale of 1-10, how are your current *OBSTACLES* affecting your life?

1 - 2 - 3 - 4 - 5 - 6 - 7 - 8 - 9 - 10

2. Who are the people who have contributed to your *OBSTACLES*? Who will you choose to help you move forward, and who will you kick to the curb, lol?

3. What is your I DECIDE statement about your *OBSTACLES*?

Write down your power statement below. Get specific!

4. When your *OBSTACLES* are eliminated, how do you expect to feel different? Do you feel healthier? Happier? More successful?

5. Where will this decision take you? Envision your life in five years and be specific.

6. Why is removing your *OBSTACLES* so important to you?

~ 7 ~
Circle of Trust

"If you surround yourself with love and the right people, anything is possible."
- **Adam Green**

We should be obligated to look at those around us in our everyday lives and see how it is affecting us, leading us, or possibly even holding us back.

Take a quick moment and think of the people you spend the most time with. These are the people you have chosen to take on the world with. As Jim Rohn says, "You're the average of the five people you spend the most time with." The fact is, some of the closest people to you could be holding you back. Our job is to shed light on your current circle of influence and help you decide whether they are helping you or hurting you. Sound harsh? It might be time. Think back to when you may have met your friends for happy hour or coffee, and the light-hearted conversations take a turn, leaving you uncomfortable and sometimes feeling disconnected. Some sitting at the table bring smiles and laughter and lift you up on your journey, while others at the very same table bring negative energy and leave you feeling uncertain and yucky.

It is time to get up from the table and recognize the patterns and behaviors of the people you are spending time with. It may be time to reevaluate the amount of time you put into certain toxic feelings and relationships. Sometimes it means not getting together or limiting time with that group to protect your heart. Learn not to be afraid, to walk away from the conversations that hurt you.

Maybe you have outgrown certain people on your current journey, and spending less time with them would be healthier. We grant you permission to feel this way. Your heart has already been telling you this, but your mind keeps saying, *Well, maybe next time it will be different.* Stop it, friend. You deserve to be surrounded by a chosen circle of people who lift you up and put sunshine in your world. No settling. We are done with that.

Now, the next question is, who should be in your circle? Kent Ingle from Home Podcast blog talks about a rowing team offering a unique depiction of team building and mentorship. They demonstrate what a team can look like when all members work as one. This makes us think, *Make sure everyone in your boat is rowing and not drilling holes when you're not looking*—know your circle. We decided to surround ourselves with a support system to create our own rowing team of life, and we want to share with you some of the best ways to choose your own team.

The first person to look for is a mentor. Find a mentor who has achieved what you are after and ask for their help and commitment.

The next step is to declutter in a very gentle way. Sometimes we need to declutter the negative thinkers and talkers from daily life. Limit your time with them to short visits. This does not mean eliminating all negative thinkers because some might be family. But be sure to choose wisely how much time you allow with them in your world. It's protection for you. It's protection from the draining feeling that negativity can cause, and it keeps you in a tip-top state of thriving and doing your best work. One way to do this is to ask yourself how you feel after you leave the presence of people. Do you feel uplifted and charged to do great things after you have been with them? Or is it the opposite? Do they drain you and bring you down? It's so important to take inventory of this for the sake of your own dreams and goals.

Next, be on the lookout for all the "cheerleaders" and communicate with those people as often as possible.

Another step is to "act as if" and rehearse as the new you. The best way to be the person you want to be is to act like you're already there.

Here's a funny story. When I was pregnant with our first child, we were given all of these beautiful gifts that felt so magical and foreign in our current lives. We used to push the baby buggy around inside our house and look at ourselves in the mirror as we passed to see what we would look like as parents. It sounds so silly that we were acting "as if" and visualizing ourselves as parents.

Are you acting "as if" you are at the levels you are trying to achieve? Is your posture as tall as the goals you have set? Are you working hard enough for the position you are running toward? This is the same for when you want to change an area of your life. Visualize yourself as healthy and strong. Speak it into your day as if you have already hit your goals. Speak to others like you are already at the next level of achievement.

Picture it with us. What if you could surround yourself with those who are where you want to be financially, physically and mentally? Their vision is so much bigger than the vision you could ever imagine for yourself. Allow them to breathe their highest standards and their biggest dreams into you daily until you believe them yourself. People who have the habits and disciplines that back up and support the activities it takes to achieve their biggest dreams and goals are the people you want surrounding you. We thrive when we can physically sit in a room with people pushing us to grow and moving us out of our comfort zone. Choose this group. Don't ever get caught being the smartest person in a room.

Ok, friends! Do you feel the weight lifted off your shoulders? You now have the power to choose your circle of influence and know anything is possible when you surround yourself with greatness.

CIRCLE OF TRUST Reflection

1. On a scale of 1-10, how is your current *CIRCLE* affecting your life?

    1 - 2 - 3 - 4 - 5 - 6 - 7 - 8 - 9 - 10

2. Who are the people currently in your *CIRCLE,* and who will you choose to move in and out of your circle from here forward?

3. What is your I DECIDE statement about your *CIRCLE OF TRUST*?

    Write down your power statement below. Get specific!

4. When your *CIRCLE* shifts, how do you expect to feel different? Do you feel healthier? Happier? More successful?

5. Where will this decision take you? Envision your life in five years and be specific.

6. Why is your *CIRCLE* shift important to you?

~ 8 ~
No Drama Mama!

"You can't control how other people behave. You can't control everything that happens to you. What you can control is how you respond to it all. In your response is your power."
- **Author Unknown**

It is inevitable, friends, that life will throw us all some crazy stuff. It is called the roller coaster of life for a reason. We twist, we turn, we even get flipped upside down. But it is how we choose to react to those moments that can be pivotal to our success. We are all climbing the mountains of life, and we will all face surprises along the way.

This hits deep in our hearts. Many people only see where we are currently in our careers but don't often see or hear the journey of defeat, trials, setbacks and sometimes tears that it took to get where we are today.

So let's talk about ways to respond to hard things and get past disappointments and tragedies with a bulletproof vest and a helmet of steel. Here are some strategies you can use when you have situations that get in the way of your ultimate goals.

Number one: Open your eyes wide and look at all aspects of the situation. How dire is it? Are you being dramatic? Is it temporary? Be realistic and calm about whether it should or could actually throw you off track from your destination or goal. Try to keep a level mind and the drama out of it, and ask a lot of questions. Some of the most successful people we know are that way because they ask many questions and have learned to become problem solvers. They don't spend much time worrying about the problem; they immediately jump into problem-solving mode.

Number two: The next thing is to outline the action steps to solve the problem. Many use what is called a Daily Method of Operations. These are non-negotiables that move you forward toward your goal. But the key is to continue with your Daily Method of Operation that you have established and not wander off course. How do you continue to work on your plan when things go bad? It's all a matter of putting one foot in front of the other, using your action steps, keeping a clear mind, a good attitude, and being persistent and disciplined.

For example, if you're working on your personal happiness, then your Daily Method of Operation, or non-negotiables, may include journaling, prayer, quiet time, exercise, and visualization. These are all things you can do every single day. And the key is not to stop when life gets busy or interrupted. That is when you need this the most. And sadly, it is the first thing people drop at the first sign of trouble.

Number three: The next major step in keeping yourself on track during harder times is adjusting and controlling your thoughts. It is natural to have doom and gloom in your brain when things go awry, but we have to choose what thoughts we allow. The adage "the sky is falling, the sky is falling" serves no one well.

Speak confidently to yourself daily: *I will get through this. I am learning from this situation. I have the strength and faith to endure all things, and this too shall pass.*

As leaders, we have mastered the art of knowing when it is time to fill our own cups to keep the bad or less productive thoughts out of our minds. We can confidently say we are perfectly imperfect, just like you.

Number four: When tracking yourself in the process, be aware. When you see a dip or a low point, acknowledge it, release it and jump right back on track. Don't let your tracking stop just because your activity or success rate is lower. We must always track to see our progress, and sometimes the low points lead and redirect us to a higher place where we have never been.

For example, if you've decided to get your finances in order this year and something "extra" pops up that may not be in your budget but you desperately want it anyway, accept the setback and acknowledge that you're allowed to have some fun. Track it, write it down, and find a way the following month to save in other areas. That might mean eating dinner at home the following week or skipping your fancy coffees. But whatever it takes, your response includes no guilt, no shame. It is full of self-love and appreciation for the goal and decided pattern you are on. You must learn to work with things like this that might change throughout your journey. Remember, it is never a straight road.

In business, as in sports, we win some and we lose some. But as a coach and a mentor, we don't ever throw in the towel. We huddle our team, acknowledge our setbacks and fumbles, adjust for the next play, the next day, and move forward.

As leaders in the sales industry, we have learned that this is one of the hardest but most important tools for any sales business. A salesman has to understand that there will be ups and downs, and there will be many moments where sickness, deaths, natural disasters, and unplanned events will get in the way of their daily activities. And then, they will have to find a way around those roadblocks or moments of distraction, grief, or loss to help them jump back on track. It's human nature to feel devastation, hurt and pain in many life situations, but it is all in how we respond to them.

We would love to share the inspiring story of our beautiful friend Tanya and how she learned to walk through the hardest moments of anyone's life—the loss of a child.

On April 7, 2007, at 4:20 a.m., our four-year-old daughter, Nadja, passed away in the middle of the night in my arms from what was later determined to be a heart infection called myocarditis. After burying our daughter, I had to start a new position with the company the following week.

Driving to work one day, I was overwhelmed with anger and was having a very intense and not very respectful conversation with God. Let's say I was definitely in my anger phase of grieving as I was driving and letting God have it. The word "thankful" kept coming into my thoughts. He requested that every day when I drive to the city for work, I would verbally say one thing I was thankful for regarding my daughter's life.

I will never forget my first day. It was not pleasant. My words were, "God, thank you for bringing her home while she was in my arms. She could have been taken away by some evil, like a kidnapping, but you allowed me to hold her safely when she took her last breath. She left this world in my arms the same way she entered this world. I thank you for that, God."

Every day for the next two weeks, I would thank Him for something new regarding her life. It took me to a different place of grief. It transitioned me into healing. Although there was still a long way to go, it pushed me to dig deeper into God's promise, his promise of eternity.

I had many lows during this process of grieving. One that would leave me lying on my kitchen floor, crying, with no energy to pick myself up. When driving, having the sudden urge to take the left turn to the cemetery to dig up my daughter's grave so I could hold her again. I spent many nights crying alone so my other children wouldn't hear me. I contemplated taking my life so that I could be with her. I stayed as close as I could to God's promise. However, there were many times that my anger would take me somewhere else. I was a very good mother who made it a life purpose to raise a family. "Why me? Why us? Why our child?" There are so many things about that night. It is almost too much to touch. I have come a long way in my grieving. I am not sure it ever ends, but it changes. It softens. The sting doesn't completely debilitate you. Over time, the memories of that night, the horrific sound, smell, and trauma you endure fade away. You start to speak to the memories that are forever beautiful, and you will find yourself sharing those more often and smiling. When you hear others talk about her, she becomes life again, not just her death. And that is beautiful, just like she was.

Along the way, I have met many parents who have lost a child. It is helpful to talk about your loss with others who have experienced some horrible loss. It is a club you never want to be a part of, but when you are, there is beauty in supporting each other. I read a lot of books that would give me hope, which became my favorite word in the Bible. To then be told later that Nadja's name means "hope." God always gives you nuggets of hope in your life. I work hard at recognizing those sweet gifts.

If we looked at situations as what we can and cannot control, we might handle them differently. We can't control the economy, which might affect our jobs. As we heard in Tanya's story, we can't control someone's health, but it affects our lives. So many factors we cannot control, but we can control our reactions.

Tanya's strength and her daily decision to move forward brought her to a place she never thought she would be again. We are grateful for these hopeful words and pass them on to you. Keep going, dear friends. You are not alone. So often, our childhood determines our success, our wealth, our circle of influence, our happiness, our health, and how we respond to these things. But this is your choice. You are in charge of your future and no one else: not your parents, not your environment, not your boss, not your peers. No. It is up to you.

Our friend and mentor, Justin, shares his story of the moment he reacted to a pivotal time in his childhood.

I remember when I was twelve years old, and my parents were going through a divorce. It was an emotional time. My dad was moving out, and my mom was so stressed trying to figure out how she would provide for our family.

I was the oldest kid at home in my mom's house, and we lived in this goofy rental place, a kind of dungeon and a yucky place. There were a lot of heightened emotions. I remember sitting in school. I was just a kid. I was in 7th grade at the beginning of something great. I was in math class. I can remember the teacher talking, and I was literally tuned out. I could see his lips moving, but I couldn't hear any words. I looked out the window and thought, "What am I going to do with my life?" And I remember thinking to myself, "I can have sex with girls, I can drink alcohol, I can do drugs, I can do whatever the heck I want. And for the rest of my life, I can blame my parents." I could be a rebel and just say, "Screw you guys!" It was like I had a little devil on one shoulder telling me I could do whatever I wanted. And then I had a little angel on the other shoulder, saying, "Okay, that's true. You can do that if you want. You can even blame your parents if you want." But all I heard from that angel was, "You have to go live that life. All of the decisions you make, you're totally welcome to make them. You can blame everyone else, but you're the one who has to pay the price."

I decided to take personal responsibility for my life, take accountability, not blame others, and not be the victim of what I was ready to blame on the divorce. That twelve-year-old kid would be proud to know that I chose the path of being devoted to one woman. Drugs and alcohol have never been a part of my rhythm, which all stemmed from that decision. With two choices on my shoulders, I decided to take ownership versus blaming everyone else.

Imagine how that one decision could have changed the course of Justin's life. Justin's path has led him to become an international speaker, author, and family man, all while leading many thousands of people who have experienced his wealth of expertise.

From this day forward, how will you choose to react to the twists and turns of life? Will you decide to empower your reactions to catapult you to greatness? We challenge you to use these strategies and decide to be happier, healthier and wealthier on your life's path.

REACTION Reflection

1. On a scale of 1-10, how are your current *REACTIONS* affecting your life?

1 - 2 - 3 - 4 - 5 - 6 - 7 - 8 - 9 - 10

2. Who are the people who have contributed to your *REACTIONS*? Who will you choose to help you move forward, and who will you kick to the curb, lol?

3. What is your I DECIDE statement about your *REACTION*?

Write down your power statement below. Get specific!

4. When your *REACTIONS* shift, how do you expect to feel different? Do you feel healthier? Happier? More successful?

5. Where will this decision take you? Envision your life in five years and be specific.

6. Why is your *REACTION* shift important to you?

~ 9 ~
That's A Wrap

"What feels like the end is often the beginning."
- **J.R.R. Tolkien**

Before we finish, let's go back to where we started. Our life journeys, both separately and together, over many years, brought us to one day sitting by the pool and realizing together that we had a mission and a duty to share with others that your personal decisions can change your life. We felt it in our soul to share how *YOU* can be the answer *YOU* have been waiting for. We are beyond grateful that you have taken this journey with us to empower yourself to make those decisions. This entire process has been humbling, brought belly laughs, countless tears, and (more than anything else) possibly one of the most rewarding projects we have ever done. We are the first to say that we are perfectly imperfect, but we have been called to be servant leaders, and we hope that this book has served you to make even one major decision. Change and growth are a daily grind, and we hope you will continue to walk with us, run with us at times, and get up fast when you stumble or fall along the way. Let's make this the beginning.

One day, we hope to be lying by the pool with you, sharing how this book served you and the decision you made for yourself.

We are forever grateful to our mentors for leading us on our successful path in life and to our friends and confidants for sharing their stories that moved us with every word.

To our husbands who supported this movement and this idea and are constantly pushing us to be better, and to each other, for making each other laugh until we cry, for countless hours on the phone and zoom, and for our friendship and partnership to change the world together.

The I DECIDE movement is here!

THANK YOU FOR READING OUR BOOK!

DOWNLOAD YOUR FREE GIFTS

Just to say thanks for buying and reading our book, we would like to give you a few free bonus gifts, no strings attached!

To Download Now, Visit:
www.IDecideBook.com/Freegifts

We appreciate your interest in our book, and value your feedback as it helps us improve future versions of this book. We would appreciate it if you could leave your invaluable review on Amazon.com with your feedback. Thank you!

Made in the USA
Coppell, TX
11 May 2023